Gazoduc TQM

Gazoduc TQM

Noverco

andré dubois
+ associés
designers inc.

1550 Docteur Penfield, Bureau 1405
Montréal, Québec, H3G 1C2
(514) 935-9303

Martin D
Bureau affilié
3-5 rue du Soleil-Levant
Veille-ville
1204 Genève, Suisse

Photo: Richard Cheek

Allan Greenberg, Architect

85 Willow Street
New Haven, Connecticut 06511
(203) 776-2006

1321 Connecticut Avenue, N.W.
Washington, DC 20036
(202) 785-4591

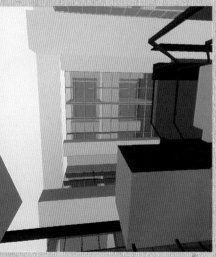

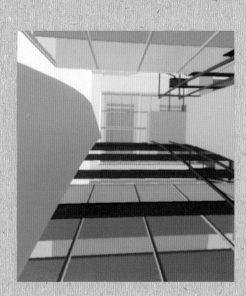
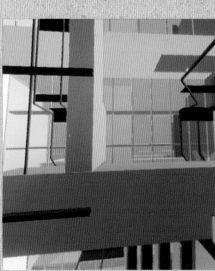

INSTANT

GRATIFICATION:

*OUR CLIENTS
SEE SOLUTIONS
AND MULTIPLE "WHAT-IFS."*

*PROVIDING
CADD-SUPPORTED
ARCHITECTURE AND
INTERIOR DESIGN.*

ALAN GAYNOR & COMPANY, P.C.
434 BROADWAY, N.Y., N.Y. 10013
212•334•0900

CORPORATE

FOREWORD

Traditionally, contracting the services of an architect or designer was done exclusively through a system of personal referrals. INTERIOR DESIGN FORUM is an extension and reinforcement of this referral system of matching designer and client. Today, thanks to publishing, greater numbers of people have greater access to the best in design.

On the pages of this, the second edition of INTERIOR DESIGN FORUM, is material on some of the best design talent in North America. Some names will be familiar, some will not; the work speaks for itself. Outstanding photography and state of the art graphic design showcases these architects and designers in a manner that is informative and inspiring.

INTERIOR DESIGN FORUM is a sourcebook in the sense that it provides information and ideas. But it is more than that. It is a celebration of the architects and designers whose work appear on these pages, and it is a tribute to the clients who commissioned the work.

CONTENTS

CONTENTS

CONTENTS

CONTENTS

**A publication of
Concept Publications Inc.**

KENNETH E. BANNON, PRESIDENT

Marketing Director:
KELLY RUDE

Marketing Representatives:
JOSEPH E. KAKNES
HERBERT J. WOSTREL

Business Administrator:
BONNIE L. BURKE

Production Managers:
CATHY GALE
KEN PFEIFER

Book Design and Production:
STEPHEN BRIDGES, BRIDGES DESIGN

Cover and Section Pages Design:
STEPHEN BRIDGES

Front and Back Matter Compiled by:
KEN PFEIFER, CONCEPT PUBLICATIONS

Typesetting:
YVONNE SWARTZ TYPESETTING
DON DEWSNAP TYPOGRAPHIC SERVICES, INC.
GRAPH PRO

ISBN 935603-48-4

Published annually by
CONCEPT PUBLICATIONS INC.
A ROCKPORT COMPANY
P.O. BOX 712, 5 SMITH STREET
ROCKPORT, MASSACHUSETTS 01966
TEL (508) 546-9401
FAX (508) 546-7141

**Distributed to the book trade and
art trade in the U.S. and Canada by:**
NORTH LIGHT, AN IMPRINT OF WRITER'S DIGEST BOOKS
1507 DANA AVENUE
CINCINNATI, OHIO 45207
TEL (513) 984-0717
FAX (513) 531-4744

**Distributed to the book trade and
art trade throughout the rest of the world by:**
HEARST BOOKS INTERNATIONAL
105 MADISON AVENUE
NEW YORK, NEW YORK 10016
TEL (212) 481-0355
FAX (212) 481-3826

Other distribution by:
ROCKPORT PUBLISHERS, INC.
5 SMITH STREET
ROCKPORT, MASSACHUSETTS 01966
TEL (508) 546-9590
FAX (508) 546-7141

INTERIOR
DESIGN FORUM

CONCEPT PUBLICATIONS

Photographies: Pierre-Louis Mongeau

Société de promotion du Centre
de Commerce Mondial de Montréal

andré dubois
+ associés
designers inc.

1550 Docteur Penfield, Suite 1405
Montréal, Quebec, H3G 1C2
(514) 935-9303

Martin D
Affiliated firm
3-5 rue du Soleil-Levant
Vieille-ville
1204 Genève, Switzerland

ANSCHUETZ, CHRISTIDIS & LAUSTER
ARCHITECTS

NEFICIOS DE SALUD

Anschuetz, Christidis and Lauster opened their office in 1983 after five years together at I.M. Pei and Partners. Today ACL is a ten member firm providing a full range of architectural services. They have built projects in New York, Boston and Washington, D.C. These projects vary from apartment renovations to new houses, from small office installations to entire commercial floors, from restaurants to schools. Their broad experience enables them to meet today's challenges with innovative solutions and high quality design.

The Chung Pak Building in New York's Chinatown is the firm's largest project to date. It is a three story base of community services and retail stores upon which will stand a low income, elderly housing tower. Chung Pak is slated for construction in 1990.

Typical recent commercial projects include a cardiology clinic, a block of new shop fronts, a series of union offices in New York, and new offices for a law firm in Boston. In a typical office project the firm works from initial programming through design and construction administration to contract furnishing. The interiors department continues to support clients' needs after the initial project is completed.

Anschuetz, Christidis and Lauster is a Minority & Women Owned Business certified with the State of New York.

104 WEST 27TH STREET, NEW YORK, NEW YORK 10001
TELEPHONE 212-691-1711
FAX 212-691-1373

Beyer
Blinder
Belle
Interiors

Since its inception, BBB Interiors has been committed to design excellence, shaping contemporary work environments to meet client needs for corporate, institutional, historic and retail interiors.

**Della Femina,
McNamee WCRS
New York City**

Corporate offices for this major advertising firm occupy the top three floors of a former manufacturing loft building. Programming the 92,500 square feet of space for a growing firm required extremely efficient use of the existing area. A dynamic environment - the laboratory for this creative agency - was developed by using a palette of textured paints, aniline-dyed woods, and glazed steel sash clerestories.

**CBS Offices and
Broadcast Center
New York City**

BBB Interiors designed over 150,000 square feet of interior office space for CBS, from 40,000 square foot floors with separate studios, editing rooms, and production offices, to personalized executive suites, lobbies, and conference areas. An extensive research program was undertaken to analyze construction systems, finishing materials, and lighting systems that would provide maximum durability and energy conservation.

22

South Street Seaport
Museum Block
New York City

The award-winning Museum Block is comprised of 13 historic buildings of various architectural styles, dating between 1790 and 1910. Cannon's Walk, formerly a series of rear yards and alleys, has been converted into a charming retail enclave. The unique character of the interior retail spaces is typified by the Seaport Bookstore where a warm and relaxed atmosphere is created by rich wood finishes and indirect lighting.

Barneys New York,
The Women's Store
New York City

Spacious and light-filled, the urbane and stylish Barneys Women's Store is the largest women's store built in New York in over 50 years. Its art deco oval staircase sweeps up six stories - with individual boutiques surrounding the staircase on each floor - to a frosted glass skylight. A two-story atrium overlooks a terrazzo fountain and cafe. The store was created by the conversion of six 1880's brownstones, their facades serving as the storefront.